WICCA

LIVING A
MAGICAL LIFE

*A Guide to Initiation and Navigating Your
Journey in the Craft*

LISA CHAMBERLAIN

Wicca Living a Magical Life

Copyright © 2016 by Lisa Chamberlain.

Published by **Chamberlain Publications (Wicca Shorts)**

ISBN-13: 978-1-912715-16-9

Disclaimer

YOUR FREE GIFT

Thank you for adding this book to your Wiccan library! To learn more, why not join Lisa's Wiccan community and get an exclusive, free spell book?

The book is a great starting point for anyone looking to try their hand at practicing magic. The ten beginner-friendly spells can help you to create a positive atmosphere within your home, protect yourself from negativity, and attract love, health, and prosperity.

Little Book of Spells is now available to read on your laptop, phone, tablet, Kindle or Nook device!

To download, simply visit the following link:

www.wiccaliving.com/bonus

GET THREE
FREE AUDIOBOOKS
FROM LISA CHAMBERLAIN

Did you know that all of Lisa's books are available in audiobook format? Best of all, you can get **three audiobooks completely free** as part of a 30-day trial with Audible.

Wicca Starter Kit contains three of Lisa's most popular books for beginning Wiccans, all in one convenient place. It's the best and easiest way to learn more about Wicca while also taking audiobooks for a spin! Simply visit:

www.wiccaliving.com/free-wiccan-audiobooks

Alternatively, *Spellbook Starter Kit* is the ideal option for building your magical repertoire using candle and color magic, crystals and mineral stones, and magical herbs. Three spellbooks —over 150 spells—are available in one free volume, here:

www.wiccaliving.com/free-spell-audiobooks

Audible members receive free audiobooks every month, as well as exclusive discounts. It's a great way to experiment and see if audiobook learning works for you.

If you're not satisfied, you can cancel anytime within the trial period. You won't be charged, and you can still keep your books!

CONTENTS

INTRODUCTION

Whether it's due to the strong connection to the natural world, the enchanting mysteries of magic, or the sense of reconnecting to the ancient deities of pre-Christian times, people from all walks of life have found themselves drawn to learning more about what is commonly referred to as "the Craft."

For some, this interest is a passing fancy, or simply one of many destinations on a lifelong itinerary of spiritual exploration. Others instantly recognize the Craft as the obvious answer to something they've been searching for their whole lives, and never waver in their passion and enthusiasm for pursuing this spiritual path.

Still others fall somewhere in between. They feel called, somehow, to Witchcraft, but they're not quite sure what to do about it. They may "dabble" in nature worship and magic when they feel so inspired, but remain stalled when it comes to truly adopting the Craft as a way of life.

If you're reading this book, odds are that Witchcraft is more than a temporary interest for you, even if you're unsure about what your interest means. You're also likely to have wondered about how to formalize your commitment to the Craft—known in Witchcraft circles as "*initiation*". But what does that really mean?

Traditionally, initiation was associated purely with covens. In the first few decades of the rise of modern Witchcraft, covens were really the only option for learning and practicing what became known as "the Old Religion." One had to be initiated into a coven to fully access all of the knowledge its members held, and usually had to take an oath of secrecy so that the teachings and practices remained hidden from outsiders.

These days, of course, anyone can learn about and practice the Craft on their own, in a uniquely personal way. Some still assert that you can only be a "Witch" if you've been initiated by another, already-initiated Witch in a formal ceremony, but this is only true in covens following a traditional path like Gardnerian Wicca.

Outside of coven practices, there is no barrier to entry into this rich and diverse way of life. Those who practice solitary and eclectic forms embrace other kinds of initiation, which may or may not involve an actual ritual. And anyway, no one holds the power to determine whether another person is entitled to identify as a Witch— this decision is up to each individual.

Self-initiation (often called self-dedication) is now a widespread and respected tradition among Wiccans and other Witches, and can be a very affirming, and even life-changing experience.

It's an act of declaration to the Universe that you fully embrace your belief and participation in the Craft. It's an affirmation of your continued exploration and learning, and of your welcoming the blessing and assistance of the gods, the spirits, the energy, or however you describe your relationship with the seen and unseen manifestations of All That Is.

So how do you decide whether to formally enact this milestone? It's really up to you, but it's highly advisable to take your time and learn as much as you can about the Craft, until you're really getting a feel for your own personal path.

Initiation doesn't mean anything if you don't yet have a clue what you're doing, regardless of how interested you may be. A ritual is not going to suddenly catapult you into a full-blown magical existence, or guarantee that you'll stay on this particular path forever.

Throughout your life, it will be up to you to continue choosing the path, in your own way and at your own pace. You may initiate into one tradition but then decide to explore others. You may self-dedicate to the path you've been discovering, but end up practicing years later in an entirely different way, from an enhanced perspective that you can only gain over time. You may even ultimately decide to join magical forces with others in a coven of compatible fellow Witches.

Really, initiation can be a range of experiences—many solitary Witches describe being "initiated by the gods" in an unplanned, unexpected way, through signs or signals, epiphanies, or other experiences of communion with the unseen. This can occur as a single event or a series of them. Some Witches are gradually "initiated" over time, as their practice continues to deepen. Others might experience successive "initiation" events throughout their lives.

Indeed, even if you never undertake an initiation or self-dedication ritual, this doesn't mean you can't be a Witch—only you know who you really are.

This guide can be of use as part of your study as you make your way toward self-initiation or self-dedication, and will include further discussion of these options, along with an example ritual you can follow or adapt to suit your preferences. But the information here is intended to be valuable regardless of whether you choose a formal entrance into the Craft.

First, we'll examine some of the potential obstacles to stepping fully and decisively onto the path, and offer possibilities for moving past them. Then we'll take a look at the basic characteristics of the initiation process in both traditional covens and solitary forms of Witchcraft. Finally, we'll close with some ideas for integrating the practice of your path more fully into your daily life.

So whether you're just beginning to learn about Witchcraft, or have been "dabbling" for some time without quite finding a solid footing, you'll find something in this guide to aid you on your way. As you read, please keep an open mind, while staying in touch with your intuition. And as with any other spiritual resource, take what you need and leave the rest.

Blessed Be.

PART ONE

FINDING YOUR WAY

WALKING YOUR PATH

The word "path" is often used in reference to religion and spirituality, whether the subject is Christianity, Buddhism, Paganism, or any number of contemporary "New Age" belief systems. A person doing any kind of spiritual seeking is said to be "on the path" of that particular pursuit, whether it involves sitting in a church, meditating in a sanctuary, practicing yoga, lighting a candle, or reading a book.

This choice of phrase, "the path," is interesting.

It is not a *road*, which exists merely to get us from one place to another as quickly as possible, and where we can be slowed down, stopped, or rushed forward by the traffic of other people making their way toward their own destinations. It is a *path*, that winds and meanders in various directions in a quiet, leisurely way, allowing us to observe our surroundings at our own pace, unhurried and unimpeded by others.

On a path, the journey is completely our own, and there is no end-goal of a particular destination. The journey *is* the destination, and therefore we are always in the right place, even when it doesn't particularly feel like it.

"The path" is a good metaphor for the study and practice of Witchcraft, as it brings to mind images of walking in nature, whether the path leads through a forest, over the crest of a mountain, through a patch of desert, or along a vast, open stretch of coastline.

When we walk on a literal, physical path, our feet are on the ground, connected to the Earth. We are breathing fresh air and moving our bodies, interacting with the energies of nature. We feel alive and awake, and open to new discoveries around every bend. We can take note of the presence of animals, insects, clouds, breezes, sunshine, rocks, leaves, the sound of water rushing along a stream or of bird calls from the tallest branches of trees.

Likewise, as we advance along our path in the Craft, we can begin to interpret what we see, hear, feel and smell in the natural world as messages to our inner selves.

We have an inherent sense that we are part of something much larger than ourselves, something more significant than the small worries and annoyances of daily life. We have gratitude for being in the moment we're in, and a pleasant sense of expectation that the next moment will also be a good moment.

This is a great state of mind to be in, because it puts us in a perfect place to manifest positive experiences in our lives. In other words, we're poised to work some excellent magic. If only we could be in this state all the time!

The truth is, we can get there much more often than we think, even if we don't currently have the ability to take leisurely hikes through nature on a regular basis. We can still find these moments on our individual paths in our ordinary daily lives.

When we allow our lives to work with the natural rhythms of the Universe, pay attention to signs and signals, and maintain a practice of tending to our spiritual selves, we are walking our path. We are learning and growing from every experience, and deepening our understanding of, and ability to work successfully with, the powerful and magical energies of nature.

Sounds inspiring, doesn't it? And yet, this path can be really elusive at times.

COMMON CHALLENGES FOR ASPIRING WITCHES

For many beginning Witches, and even for plenty of those who have been practicing for years, the sense of being on a spiritual path can seem impossible to access in the midst of the hustle and bustle of modern life.

Studying and practicing the Craft is often relegated to the category of "leisure time," something to indulge in once the work day is over and all of the chores are done. For those who have initiation or self-dedication as a goal, it may seem like there's never enough time or energy for truly engaging in sufficient study. And even for those who aren't working toward a particular benchmark like initiation, finding the motivation to keep learning and practicing can still be a challenge.

So what can you do, if you're feeling yourself to be in a stuck place regarding your own path? The first thing to do is recognize that it's okay to be stuck.

Getting frustrated with yourself over where you are is never helpful—the energy of frustration doesn't manifest positive change. Not only does it keep you stuck, but it actually deepens the ruts that your "wheels" are spinning in.

So if you feel yourself to be stuck in a rut with your wheels spinning, then the first thing to do is get out of the car. It's not a road, remember? It's a path. Your path.

You're the only one on it, so you can stop whenever you want to, or need to—for as long as you want or need to. And you can trust that when you're ready, you'll resume walking at your own pace.

You can also remind yourself that plenty of people struggle with their paths—in fact, there's not a Witch in history who hasn't experienced some kind of block within their practice, for one reason or another.

Many people would argue that the whole point of being human is to experience obstacles and then grow by either overcoming them or learning to work with them. Witches can certainly be said to have an edge when it comes to navigating obstacles through the use of magic, but we all face difficulties, regardless of spiritual orientation.

Below, we'll take a look at some of the common challenges that would-be adept Witches encounter when it comes to moving beyond the mere reading of books and into the actual practice of the Craft. You'll also find some suggestions for navigating these challenges so you can continue to move along your path, at your own desired pace.

INFORMATION OVERLOAD

The first potential obstacle, ironic though it may seem, is the unprecedented amount of information about Witchcraft for anyone interested in the subject to take advantage of. Websites, books, magazines, videos, podcasts—you name it, it's out there.

In addition to the sheer volume, the *variety* of information can also be astonishing, since under the umbrella term of "Witchcraft" there are several distinctly different branches, including Wicca and its many different traditions, various forms of Traditional Witchcraft, and all kinds of eclectic practices that borrow from several older traditions at once.

And as a result of the dramatic rise in popularity of Wicca and Witchcraft in general in recent decades, new forms of the Craft are emerging all the time, generating still more new information. It really can be quite overwhelming.

In fact, some people who want to explore this territory find the vast scope of possible choices to be too much, unable to settle on a starting point. Others might spend some time collecting a shelf full of books on Witchcraft and other occult topics, and maybe even acquire a few magical tools, but find themselves unsure about their choices, and therefore unable to really "get into it" when it comes to developing a regular practice.

And then there's the related issue of conflicting information. Many aspiring Witches can get stuck when two or more sources they really respect describe vastly different approaches to a particular element of practice, such as how to begin a ritual. Indeed, it seems that one of the very qualities that draws many to the world of the Craft—the lack of rigid structures or uniform, standard procedures—can also be a challenge when it comes to finding your way in.

The good news is that most people who are interested in Witchcraft tend to be independent thinkers and have a strong connection to their own intuition. These traits can serve you well when it comes to navigating the maze of voices, perspectives, ideas and assertions that you're bound to encounter when researching the Craft.

The more you pay attention to your intuitive responses to what you read or hear—including emotional and physical responses—the more quickly you learn to discern between ideas that resonate and information that, for whatever reason, just doesn't speak to you.

So no matter how new you are to the subject of Witchcraft, remember to trust your own judgement and the signals that your higher self sends you. Read the books and websites that catch your interest, and give a pass to those that don't.

It's true that as you're setting out on your journey, you should read about a variety of perspectives and possible pathways, whether it be Wicca or other forms of Witchcraft—or both. But you can't possibly read everything, so don't exhaust yourself trying.

And don't ever feel obligated to take on another person's perspective on the Craft simply because they're emphatic about it. You may not have the level of experience that the author of a book or website has—you may, in fact, have none at all—but you are still the ultimate authority on your individual path.

LIVING AMONG
THE UNENLIGHTENED

In addition to being independent thinkers with a strong sense of intuition, people who are drawn to Witchcraft tend to have other traits in common, like an affinity with the natural world that goes beyond simply enjoying a hike and taking photographs of wildlife. They feel a sense of communion with nature when they're in it, a presence that isn't felt in the "civilized" world of suburbs and shopping malls.

Witches have a healthy appreciation of mystery, and enjoy contemplating phenomena that can't be understood through the lens of rational thought. They are at home with the feeling that there is much more to life than what is visible on the surface, that what constitutes "reality" goes well beyond everything we've been taught in our schools and our communities.

Finally, Witches tend to have unusually sharp sixth-sense (or "psychic") capabilities, whether these talents show up as clairvoyance (picking up spiritual messages through visual images), clairaudience ("hearing" messages from spirit as an inner voice), or empathy (tuning into the feelings of others).

Often, a person will have a combination of two or more of these gifts, but one may be dominant. These abilities allow us to "just know" things without any tangible evidence, and when we recognize and trust them, they help us make good decisions and avoid trouble.

It probably goes without saying that these characteristics are not exactly prized in mainstream culture.

Although it's true that independent thinking (or "thinking outside of the box") is considered a positive attribute in the workplace in many fields, our social worlds—particularly in the United States—still overwhelmingly favor compliance with the dominant belief systems at work in our culture, whether these come from science-based "rational" thinking, one of the major world religions, or a mix of both.

In this environment, psychic abilities and a fascination with the unseen are met with suspicion, rather than enthusiasm. "Witchy types" may feel out of their element most of the time, and are unlikely to feel safe sharing their own worldview and experiences with the people around them.

Indeed, despite the above-mentioned explosion of interest in the subject over the past few decades, Witchcraft remains incredibly taboo in the majority of the English-speaking countries in which it's practiced.

Even (and perhaps especially) in the U.S., where Wicca has actually been granted official status as a religion, identifying publicly as a Witch can be incredibly risky, depending on where you live. People who are uneducated about the Craft may accuse you of "devil-worship," suspect you of illegal drug use, or decide that you must be mentally unstable.

So if you don't have any friends or family members who share your interest, or are at least tolerant of it, you may be keeping this very significant aspect of your life a total secret, with no one at all to discuss it with. It can feel a bit lonely at times, to say the least.

Of course, not everyone is in this situation. If you live in a cosmopolitan city where attitudes are liberal and "anything goes," or if you at least have friends or acquaintances in your community who share your interests, then you most likely don't have to be closeted about your identity as a Witch.

Or, you may be one of those rare people who just has absolutely no hangups whatsoever about what other people think. Perhaps you play the role of a trailblazer for the Craft in your community, using your courage and inner strength to openly pave the way for others to come out of the shadows, in which case, you are much appreciated by your fellow Witches!

But if you, like most humans, prefer as much harmony in your social and/or family life as possible, you may find that you're better off not disclosing your identity as a Witch. There's nothing wrong with this at all, but many find that it does make it a bit hard to maintain enthusiasm for consistent study and practice.

The good news is that even if you're not blessed with the presence of like-minded others in your life, there are a few things you can do to energize your desire to keep moving forward on your path.

First, know that there's really no *need* to be "out" as a Witch to anyone in your life. In fact, many traditions of Witchcraft require vows of secrecy, whether to avoid social ostracism or to honor those who came before us in prior centuries, when being known as a Witch was a very real threat to one's safety, and could even cost people their lives.

So even if you're completely solitary on your path, you're actually still in good company. And of course, on the astral plane, you're never truly alone—you can always communicate with those in the spirit world who support you in your pursuit of the Craft.

Second, you can take advantage of living in the Internet Age and do some research to find out whether there are like-minded people in your area. It's entirely possible that there are others who feel the same way you do about maintaining secrecy in the outer world, but still would like to communicate with other Witches in private. This could be in the form of a coven, or something more informal like a circle or discussion group.

And even if there's no one to meet with in person for hundreds of miles, there are definitely plenty of online groups—particularly among Wiccans, but also among other Witches—where you can connect, ask questions, share ideas, and find camaraderie with others who share your solitary plight.

Finally, the most important step—no matter what your social circumstances may be—is to own and embrace who you really are. If you feel called to the Craft, answer that call, and let the connection it fosters with your true self be the most important thing in your life.

So many people who participate in the dominant, monotheistic religions are doing so at least partly out of a perceived social obligation. ("If I don't go to church, other people will notice and then gossip about me!") In fact, so many people never get in touch with who they really are on any level, because they're too busy trying to conform to the expectations of mainstream society.

Viewed in this light, the path of the solitary, secretive Witch is perhaps the most incredibly freeing and self-validating spiritual experience available to you. After all, you're definitely not doing this for anyone but yourself!

As it happens, when you embrace your witchy self just as you are, and don't allow social or cultural prejudices to get in your way, you are much more likely to attract new people into your life who resonate with your spirituality, your personality, and your way of perceiving the world.

So focus on you and your own growth, and live from your heart. As you progress along your path, you may eventually find that you've become comfortable sharing your spiritual side with more people, which will in turn attract more like-minded people to you.

In fact, we've been seeing this phenomenon in the exponential growth of practitioners of the Craft over the past few decades. As new generations have discovered the path, we have collectively made major advances in acceptance of, and even respect for, this beautiful and creative way of life.

So be proud of your path, and of yourself for following it, regardless of whether you'd ever tell anyone in your life what you're up to.

SO MANY MOONS, SO LITTLE TIME...

Another challenge that new Witches may struggle with is not quite knowing how to integrate their spiritual and magical practice into the daily routines of their otherwise-mundane lives.

If you work 40 (or more) hours per week, or are in school, or have the responsibility of taking care of a family (or all of the above), it can be hard to feel that you even have time for reading about the Craft or engaging in a little spellwork, let alone observing the 13 full moons and 8 sabbats on the Wheel of the Year.

And if you're a solitary Witch, with no coven or circle to celebrate moons and holidays with, it can be harder to summon up the motivation to clear your calendar and devote your time and attention to these special days.

You may even find yourself putting off spellwork that you know would be beneficial to your life, because you can't see how to get yourself in the right frame of mind to make it effective. It can be quite a feat to shake off the workday sludge and allow space for that magical feeling to flow through you.

If you're feeling dispirited about not being able to build spiritual activity into your life, it's important to recognize that you don't need to take an all-or-nothing approach. Remember, it's called a path for a reason—you're supposed to take it one step at a time, and you're supposed to go at your own pace.

There are no rules about how much, or how often, or when or where or in what way to practice your Craft. But there are many small, purposeful steps you can take toward your goal of creating a more regular, consistent practice.

First of all, keep in mind that unless you are a member of a Wiccan coven that operates through participation in scheduled rituals, there is no requirement that you observe all, or any, of the full moons, solstices, equinoxes, or other festivals associated with the Wheel of the Year. If you are following a Wiccan path, then these are definitely a big component of the spiritual life, but that doesn't mean that you're doing something wrong if you don't honor every single holiday.

These times exist as opportunities to connect with the Earth, with any deities you may work with, and with the spirit energy of other Witches following a similar path in their own way. But they should be seen as opportunities rather than obligations. Whether you're practicing Wicca or some other path of the Craft, if you're going about your preparations for a sabbat or full moon ritual and feeling stressed or even a little resentful about it, then something's not right.

To allow for a more relaxed and joyful approach to celebrating whatever holidays you're able to, embrace the art of compromise.

If the Spring Equinox is coming up and you see that it falls on that Wednesday when you have a late meeting after work, then you could choose to mark it on Thursday, or even Tuesday, instead. While it's fun, and often quite powerful, to perform a ritual as close to the exact time of an equinox as possible, it's not like there's a huge amount of difference in the length of day and night between Tuesday, Wednesday, and Thursday of that week.

In other words, these holidays mark *points* on the wheel of the seasons. The purpose of observing them is to acknowledge where we are on the wheel at that time. A few days on either side of that designated point is not going to diminish the power of your intentions. You're still taking time to focus on the present moment and be in gratitude for the blessings in your life.

Of course, when it comes to timing celebrations of full and new moons, there's a little less leeway, given that the lunar cycle is so much shorter than the solar cycle. Nonetheless, if you're wanting to work some full moon magic but can't time it exactly right, go ahead and do it the night before!

If your intention is just as clear and strong as it would be on the actual night of the full moon, there's no reason to believe you won't be successful. Most people feel the energetic effects of a full moon for at least two or three days surrounding the moment when it's technically full, so why would magic only be potent at that specific time?

That's not to say that certain spells that are *designed* for exact timing with the full moon can be worked whenever you want and turn out successfully—timing is a magical tool, after all. But you can choose spellwork that isn't targeted for a specific point in time. And remember that magic has been around since long before most people had the ability to know the exact moment of a moon phase by checking their clocks. So don't put off spellwork that you really want to do simply because you can't do it at the "perfect" time.

Speaking of timing, another way of integrating Witchcraft more fully into your life is to observe the various magical correspondences between moon phases, as well as days of the week, and specific purposes.

It's generally understood that spells worked for increase (in terms of prosperity or love, for example) are best done when the moon is waxing or full, while spells worked to remove something from your life (an illness, a debt, or some other unwanted situation) are best during the waning phase.

To get even more specific, each day of the week has its ideal magical goals, based on the planet assigned to the day. Friday, associated with Venus, is the first choice for love spells, while Thursday, ruled by expansive Jupiter, is good for magic relating to money and prosperity.

If you put both of these systems together, then you can see that a Friday during a waxing moon would be the best time to work a spell for attracting a new relationship.

A Thursday during a waning moon is good for spellwork to eliminate obstacles to prosperity.

Some Witches find the daily correspondences and the moon phase considerations to be too restrictive. After all, what if you have an urgent communication-related need that you want to perform spellwork for, that isn't going to wait until two Wednesdays from now when the moon is waxing again? In fact, plenty of non-Wiccan Witches ignore the daily correspondences altogether—although most do work with the moon phases.

The truth is, you should do your spellwork when you're able and willing to, regardless of the day of the week. As always, your focus on your intention is the single most important factor in any magical working. But it's good to recognize that daily correspondences and moon phases offer opportunities to work some structure into your magical practice.

Say a sudden inspiration to do a candle spell strikes you one evening, but you feel overwhelmed by the possibilities for a specific intention. You can use the correspondences to help you decide!

If it's Saturday, and the moon is waxing, you might choose to work for increased psychic clarity. Now you've narrowed it down to a specific goal, and you know that your work for this goal has the support of the moon and the planet Saturn. And just knowing this brings an extra magical boost to your work!

Ultimately, integrating the Craft into your daily life—one step at a time, at your own pace—is the goal. The sabbats and moon cycles create an ongoing, affirming rhythm in our lives around the Wheel of the Year, but it's in our daily habits—of mind and of practice—where lasting spiritual development occurs.

There are many small, yet significant ways to gradually transform your life so that you're living a magical experience every single day, whether or not you have time for elaborate spellwork. Let's take a look at some practices you can incorporate into your daily routine that will keep your magical connection with the Universe in your daily awareness.

First and foremost, if you don't do this already, consider adopting a daily meditation practice. Witches, sages, and mystics have known for centuries what modern brain science is just now discovering—that meditation creates very powerful, positive changes in the brain that can enhance our abilities to do just about anything, and this certainly includes magic!

We tend to get overrun, without even realizing it, by unnecessary and unhelpful thoughts zooming around in our busy minds from morning until night. Almost all of these thoughts are somehow related to something in our past or a concern about our future. A daily practice of meditation helps us get better at letting go of those thoughts, allowing us to focus on what's right in front of us, which is a key component of successful magic.

You probably already know that any spellwork performed with a distracted, sped-up, "monkey" mind is quite unlikely to be successful, which is why Witches take such care to achieve a clear, relaxed, focused state of mind before beginning any ritual or other magical work.

If you're in a regular habit of meditation, you have more familiarity with this state of mind, and can achieve it more quickly and easily when it comes time to engage with the Universe on a magical level. And simply *knowing* you can get there more easily is often enough to get you past that resistant voice that says "I'm too frazzled to focus enough for magic today."

This doesn't mean that you need to sit cross-legged in the lotus position chanting "om" on a cushion for 30 minutes a day (although you'd benefit enormously in many ways if you did so!). The goal here is to develop a practice that you can stick to, so start with an amount of time that you know is manageable, even if it's as little as 5 minutes.

You can play some soothing music or meditative sounds, or even a guided meditation—all of which can be found for free online. If you have a timer on your phone or an alarm clock, you can set it for the desired length of time, so that you won't have to open your eyes to see how long you've been at it. (Try to use something that makes a gentle sound when the mediation's over—it's rather jarring to be interrupted by loud beeps or other "alarming" alarm sounds!) You'll find more tips for successful meditation at the end of this section, along with a short, simple meditation to try.

Try to meditate around the same time every day, so that your body and mind get into a rhythm with it. Once you're in a groove, start adding one minute to your timer every week or so, in order to gradually increase the length of your meditations.

A meditation practice builds its own momentum over time, so you should begin to notice differences in your anxiety levels and ability to focus after a couple of weeks. You'll also notice that you feel you have more time to pay attention to your Craft, since slowing down and centering are key elements of working with the energies of the natural world.

There are other simple ways to infuse your daily life with a more magical awareness.

You can make charm bags with your favorite crystals, herbs, and/or other ingredients and keep them in various places where you'll see them each day—such as in your kitchen and your car. You can charge your morning coffee with an affirmation or blessing, setting a positive intention for the day and truly savoring that first magical sip. You can carry crystals in your pockets during the work day, and hold them during times of stress or boredom, keeping you in touch with the magical energies of the Earth.

Crystals and other mineral stones are also great in jewelry, of course, and this is a particularly good option for people who don't want their identities as Witches to be known to those around them. You can quite openly wear an amber pendant, charged for luck, protection, or some other magical purpose, and though you'll likely get plenty of compliments on it, no one will be the wiser!

Over time, working these small practices into your daily life will create a foundation for your spiritual evolution, and help ground and center you on your path.

As you continue to learn and grow in the Craft, remember that it does take time to build a deep personal practice, and that your pace is your own. As time goes on, you'll be able to look back at the early stages of your pursuit of this path and see how much more comfortable and confident you've become, little by little. And it's more than likely that as you relax about whether or not you're marking all the moons and holidays, you will find yourself with more time and energy to celebrate these occasions.

So resist any temptation you feel to be a perfectionist about "sticking to the schedule." Don't indulge in guilty feelings about skipping your morning meditation or letting a new moon go by without lighting a candle. Approach every ritual, celebration, and magical working you're able to devote time to with an attitude of ease and joy, and trust that you're exactly where you're supposed to be in every moment.

RELIGION AND RATIONALISM: GETTING BEYOND OLD BELIEFS

For some would-be Witches, the biggest hurdle to fully embracing a life in the Craft is not their social circumstances or their busy schedules. Instead, it's the challenge of reconciling the beliefs involved in practicing Witchcraft with whatever beliefs they were brought up with, whether those are religious, rationalist, or a mix of both.

These days, more and more Witches are born into families that already practice Wicca or some other form of the Craft, and therefore begin learning about it from an early age. However, this is not the case for the vast majority of people who find themselves drawn to this way of life.

Many aspiring Witches discover the Craft as teenagers. Others are young adults or even middle-aged adults. Those who remain interested in it after reading a few sources have found ideas or beliefs that resonate with them. But the process of accepting and adopting a new belief system can still feel unclear.

LOSING YOUR RELIGION

While it seems that a majority of Witches were raised in non-religious families, or else had parents who had left their own families' religion behind, many do come to the Craft from religious backgrounds. Most were brought up in a denomination of Christianity, but other faiths are represented as well.

A religious upbringing can be tricky for an aspiring Witch, particularly for those who grew disillusioned with a faith they once followed, and especially for those whose family lives were strongly infused with their religion.

If this is your situation, you might experience resistance to much of what you read and hear about Witchcraft, no matter how much it resonates with some parts of you. This resistance might be subtle or quite active, and can come from a variety ideas that you may have consciously let go of, but are deeply ingrained nonetheless.

For example, you might struggle with adopting a new concept of deity, such as the Wiccan God and Goddess, or any of their "lesser" aspects from the various pantheons that practitioners of Wicca and other forms of the Craft follow. You may have had it instilled in you from an early age that the deity (usually known simply as "God") of your religion is the only one, and that any other deity is completely fabricated by human beings, or else somehow inappropriate to give your attention to.

Many sects of Christianity in particular have long held that anything with the slightest whiff of paganism is inherently "evil," but this idea is found within the other monotheistic religions as well. So even though you know in your heart that there's nothing wrong with following a different deity, and doing so in an entirely different way, it can still feel rather strange.

You may also have been raised with a concept of deity (usually "God") as one who is both benevolent and punishing, watching and judging your every action and providing you with plenty of opportunities to feel guilty if you're not living up to what you've been taught is the ideal standard of behavior. In this kind of belief system, a rigid concept of the afterlife is often used as motivation for keeping oneself in line, and the rules involved can run from simple to complex, and from sensible to seemingly random and bizarre.

People who leave religions with strict dogma tend to be wary of the word "god," whether it's capitalized or not, and are generally resistant to anything resembling "rules." So when you come across a Witch or a book that appears to take a dogmatic approach to the Craft (such as a fixed arrangement of the altar that must be followed consistently, or some other element of practice that can only be viewed from a specific perspective), it can be off-putting.

The concept of goddesses is also challenging for some who have been raised in the patriarchal religious systems of Judaism, Christianity, and Islam, although this is also a major draw, if not *the* major draw, for many Witches who work with deities.

The presence of a divine feminine and the balanced equality between the two genders in many forms of the Craft is a refreshing and welcoming experience for many who come from a patriarchal background. And some forms of Wicca actually leave male deities out of it altogether. Nonetheless, if your former notion of divinity was exclusively male, then goddesses can be a little hard to get used to.

Not all forms of Witchcraft recognize deities, however, and it should also be acknowledged that a vast number of Witches would reject the idea that their path is a religion. Wicca is officially recognized as a religion in many places, but even some Wiccans decline to identify it that way.

It should also be noted that there are Witches who continue to practice their religion of origin along with Witchcraft and see no conflict between the two—even if most members of that religion of origin would disagree!

If you're feeling called to the Craft, but uncertain or hesitant about how the concept of deity fits with your worldview as a "religious refugee," know that your experience of this path is yours alone.

No one can make you believe in anything, and no amount of worshiping or honoring or invoking a deity is going to make it real for you if you're just going through the motions because it seems like you're "supposed to." Unless you belong to a Wiccan coven that worships particular aspects of the Goddess and God, you really have a wide range of possibilities to explore in this department.

If following a well-established path is what feels right, then you may be more predisposed to follow deities that are widely believed in by members of specific traditions. Or you can take the "eclectic" route and build your own practice, which may or may not include deities.

No matter how your path evolves, you can let go of the idea that any one religion or belief system is the "correct" one. In fact, it can be very useful to allow for the possibility that the infinite Universe has room for *all* deities and *all* beliefs, with no one particular set of ideas being any more correct than another.

You can also relax, take your time, and trust that you will find your way when you're ready. Although some people do end up having a specific mystical or spiritual experience that immediately opens them up to a new understanding of the non-physical world in a particular and lasting way, most of us come to an understanding of our deities of choice (or lack thereof) more gradually.

So don't let mixed feelings about "religion" stop you from following your inner guidance. Know that if you listen to yourself first, you'll always end up where you're meant to be.

THAT PESKY THING CALLED "PROOF"

As mentioned earlier, people who adopt Witchcraft as a way of life are more likely than not to have been raised in non-religious families. They might describe their upbringing as "atheist," "rationalist," or simply "not religious."

There's a spectrum of belief systems represented here, from those with staunchly atheist views, many of whom will *insist* that there is no "God," and that the deities of all cultures around the globe are simply human fabrications, to agnostics, who aren't completely sure either way. (Rationalists, like atheists, reject the notion of deity, but like agnostics, tend not to feel the need to actively "take a side" in the question.)

Rationalists, by definition, take a very skeptical attitude toward unseen phenomena, whether it be paranormal activity, magic, or anything else that can't be proven to be real by some acceptable scientific standard. Atheists may very well believe in the invisible realms, but dispute the notion that any kind of deity is responsible for aiding in magical manifestations.

Of course, depending on your personal perspective, these terms may overlap. Unlike organized religions, there's no creed for atheism or rationalism, other than a belief that deities do not exist, so there's no established definition of either. And there are other terms—like "skeptic" or "humanist"—that many non-religious people identify with instead.

There are, however, plenty of Witches who identify with any number of these terms.

Atheist Witches participate in the spirit realm and practice magic, but do not, obviously, work with deities.

Rationalist Witches practice magic, but don't subscribe to the "spiritual" worldview. Instead, they understand the power to manifest as a result of the psychological effects that spellwork creates in the brain, making them more likely to focus and make choices that lead them to their goals.

Or, they may understand it as a result of the Law of Attraction, a topic which has gained plenty of currency in the last several years, even among many in the mainstream culture. Then there's the cutting-edge field of quantum physics, which has been evolving to a point where its theories can essentially be viewed as the underpinnings of how magic works.

These concepts are generally easier for many aspiring Witches with "non-mystical" worldviews to wrap their minds around. Even so, when you're new to the Craft, it can take some time to get to a place where your skeptical origins can peacefully coexist with phenomena that can't be "proven" or explained in a traditional scientific manner.

Particularly given the culture we live in, which would essentially brand you as crazy for believing in magic, it can be hard to get beyond "keeping an open mind" to truly accepting the ideas underlying your new practice on a consistent basis.

If this is your situation, you may very likely experience fluctuating confidence about choosing this path. You may have brief glimmers of an unseen force moving through you and around you in a particularly magical moment, but then wake up the next day thinking it must have just been your imagination. And if you're keeping your explorations of Witchcraft a secret from family or friends in order to avoid awkward or even contentious conversations, it can be a lonely road to solidifying your beliefs.

The trouble with this dance between skepticism and acceptance, particularly when it comes to magic, is that without real belief, you *can't* make it work. And if the spellwork you're trying doesn't get results, it has the effect of reinforcing your doubt.

This kind of block can happen no matter what kind of beliefs were instilled in you from a young age— many, if not most people from religious backgrounds also struggle with resistance from their "rationalist" beliefs. Indeed, this is a place many, many aspiring Witches find themselves in at the beginning, and it's pretty easy to get stuck here, especially if you don't have the support of others in your life who have gotten past it.

So what can you do to move through this "agnostic" phase of your path?

First of all, it's key to have patience—again, frustration doesn't get you anywhere.

Second, stay open to the same perspective offered above to those who are inhibited by their former religious beliefs: there are many, many paths to understanding and consciously participating in the grand cosmic scheme of things.

As you continue to seek your own path, remember to take it one step at a time. Keep your spellwork simple, with relatively minor or short-term goals. Candle magic is a great form for beginners, particularly because it's hard to gaze on a flickering flame without being at least a little enchanted! Try a candle spell for elevating your mood— these often have especially notable results, which will last longer and longer the more you practice.

Meditating, spending time in nature, and "unplugging" from unnecessary stimuli like television and social media will always enhance your spiritual side.

And of course, keep reading everything you can about the Craft. Become more discerning about which authors and ideas resonate with you, and discard anything that doesn't. Finding a book or a blog or a website that inspires you is often just the thing you need to open up further and expand your understanding of your path.

No matter who you are or where you're from, you really do have to transform your ingrained and often unconscious beliefs in order to accommodate a life in the Craft. This is part of the work of initiation, whether you undergo a formal ritual or not.

It could be argued that teenagers have it the easiest in this regard, since it's in the nature of people at this stage in life to explore widely as they seek to shape their identities and their way of seeing the world. They're generally quite open to new ideas and alternative perspectives.

There's also an almost electrical charge to much of life at this age, which can make perceiving unseen realities much easier. This may be at least part of why Wicca and other forms of Witchcraft are so popular with teenagers and young adults.

By contrast, many people say that the older we get, the harder it is to be open to change and to shake off long-held beliefs about how the world works. However, this isn't necessarily true. It really all depends on your particular circumstances—your upbringing, your personality, the events of your life thus far, and your openness to change in general.

But whatever your age or background, your pursuit of the Craft shows that you're not much interested in sticking to a conventional way of viewing the world. Knowing this about yourself is a good start toward feeling at home in the magical and spiritual life you're now creating.

SPELLS AND PRACTICES FOR MORE MAGICAL LIVING

In some ways, it could be argued that "path" is not exactly a perfect metaphor for the experience of bringing the Craft into one's life.

"Path" rather implies that the ground you're walking on is well-tended, that there are no forks or detours or obstacles to interrupt your smooth stroll.

In truth, this quest is more like a "trail," where there may be narrow, rocky patches or fallen trees that must be climbed over, or forks that give no indication of where you'll end up once you've chosen one direction over another.

If your chief obstacle is choosing among the seemingly infinite possibilities of beliefs and forms within the umbrella term of "Witchcraft," it may feel like you're facing several different "forks" at once. Or, you could simply be feeling lonely out there, with no one in your family or social sphere to share your interest and discoveries with.

Maybe your challenge is in integrating the time and focus it takes to advance along the path into your busy life. Or perhaps it's about getting past old, limiting beliefs about the Universe and what we have been taught to identify as "reality."

In all actuality, it's likely that each of these circumstances will affect you to some degree, at some point or another, since they are such common elements of life in the 21st century.

Fortunately, none of these obstacles can actually force you off your path—only you can decide whether or not the Craft is really for you. And though patience and persistence are key to moving forward, there are also plenty of practical steps you can take to move out of places that feel "stuck."

You'll find some examples below, in the form of meditation ideas and a bit of spellwork. Try them out and see what works for you.

And no matter what you do, keep in mind that on nature hikes—particularly the wilder, more adventurous ones—the "path" can sometimes be very faint, or even seem to disappear altogether for awhile, before it becomes clear again.

When this happens to you, keep trusting that you're still on track, as you take those tentative steps in between the visible stretches.

"PROTECTIVE BUBBLE" ENCHANTMENT

When you're spending most of your time among the "unenlightened," the path can get pretty obscured at times.

Witches tend to be very sensitive to the energetic vibrations of the people around them. This is generally considered to be a blessing, and can be marvelous when you're surrounded by positive, open-minded people.

But most of us are not so blessed as to be in this situation at all times. And when you're around people who are negative or closed-minded, it's easy to be affected by their moods and lose your connection to your witchy inner self.

This is particularly true for Witches who work in occupations that are inherently stressful, fast-paced, and/or involve interacting with the public, but it can also be an issue in one's home environment as well.

This enchantment technique helps you keep healthy boundaries around your personal energy, shielding you from the negativity of others and keeping you connected to your own spiritual power. Best of all, you can draw upon it whenever you need to throughout your day without calling attention to the fact that you're working magic!

To set up the enchantment, you'll need some time and space where you can be alone and undisturbed. This is very important, since you are creating an energetic experience that you'll be relying on when you're in the midst of people who are difficult to be around.

In other words, you need to have a solid foundation of peace and well-being to draw from. So be sure to establish a feeling of calm and serenity before you begin, perhaps by using the Reconnection Meditation exercise described below.

This enchantment connects a physical gesture to a feeling of calm, centered well-being.

Instructions:

Choose a gesture you can make with your hand that's reasonably subtle and will not draw the attention of others.

This can be anything that comes naturally to you, but commonly used examples include making a circle with your thumb and index finger, crossing your fingers, or making a fist, all of which can be done when your arms are at your sides and your hands are out of view.

You can also try tugging gently at your earlobe, or placing your palm on the back of your neck. You may want to experiment a little until you find something you're comfortable with.

Once you've chosen your gesture, close your eyes and take three deep breaths, letting go of any extraneous thoughts or concerns.

Make the gesture, and as you do, envision yourself surrounded completely by a bubble of pure white light.

Hold this vision for several moments, allowing yourself to feel completely protected and at peace. No unwanted energy from others can disturb you in this place, and nothing can come between you and your spiritual center.

When you feel a very strong connection between this feeling and the gesture you're making, you can say the following affirmation, or create one of your own:

"All is right, bright and well here in my center."

Take another deep breath, release it, and then open your eyes.

Keep holding the gesture for another deep breath or two with your eyes open, to lock in the association between the gesture and the feeling. When you feel ready, you can then release the gesture.

You have now created a powerful, portable enchantment. The next time you're in a social situation of any kind that feels uncomfortable, you can subtly make your gesture, take a conscious, focused breath, and bring that bubble of protective light immediately to your assistance.

If you like, you can repeat the affirmation silently to yourself. The more you use this enchantment, the stronger and more instantly effective it will become.

QUICK "RECONNECTION" MEDITATION

As discussed above, a regular meditation practice is highly recommended for every Witch, but especially for those who have busy schedules, as a hectic pace of life can make it quite difficult to slow down and tune in to your inner self.

This very brief meditation exercise is useful at any point in the day, but particularly when you feel disconnected from yourself due to distractions caused by others, or by stressful circumstances. Try using it as a way of transitioning from the work day to the evening, especially when you're planning to work magic and/or celebrate a holiday.

This exercise is most effective when you're sitting comfortably in a quiet place, but you can also do it "on the go" just about anywhere you happen to be. The main thing is to be paying attention to your breathing throughout the meditation.

Instructions:

Close your eyes and take a long, slow, deep breath in as you (silently) count to four.

Hold your breath for another count of four, and then gently, slowly, let it go, again to a count of four.

Then wait for another count of four before taking the second long, slow, deep breath in.

Hold for another count of four, let it go, and then wait one more count of four before opening your eyes and returning to breathing as normal.

Note that you don't have to stop after two rounds of this— you can do this exercise for as long as you like—but be sure to do at least two cycles of breathing in, holding, breathing out, and holding before opening your eyes.

When you finish, take a moment to notice how the difference in the "noise level" in your mind, as well as any other sensations that come through.

You may want to close out the meditation with an affirmation, such as *I am now reconnected with my center*, or *Blessed Be*.

TIPS FOR
THE MEDITATING WITCH

Although we generally think of meditation as an Eastern spiritual activity, there are plenty of ways to blend Western Witchcraft into your meditation practice.

You can surround yourself with crystals and/or light a candle to sit in front of during your meditation. You can also choose specific Tarot (or other divination) cards to hold and gaze at while you pay attention to your breath.

Some Witches like to concentrate on the card, then close their eyes and hold the imagery in their third eye for as long as they can. This helps slow down the "monkey mind" by providing it with a visual task.

If you have a patron deity, you can use an image of the deity in this manner as well, and in this way forge a stronger spiritual connection with the deity through your meditation.

Finally, incense or essential oils in a diffuser can enhance your mind's ability to slow down and enter an altered state. If you use incense, be sure to sit a good distance from the actual smoke so you don't inhale it as you breathe deeply.

If you've never meditated before, or if you've tried but found yourself unable to "stop thinking thoughts," don't worry!

In actuality, successful meditation does not have to be "thought-free." You will almost certainly get distracted by random, uninvited thoughts during meditation.

The trick is to let them go, rather than engaging with them. So any time you realize that you've drifted off into your to-do list again, or are replaying something that happened earlier in your day, simply let it go and return your focus to your breath.

Part of the magic of meditation is that simply *trying* to slow down your mind, no matter how successful (or unsuccessful) you are, makes a significant difference. So regardless of how distracted or scattered you're feeling as you start your meditation, know that it's never a waste of time or effort!

"SPIRIT CONNECTION" CHARM BAG

Charm bags are fun, easy ways to keep a little magic with you wherever you go. You can keep them discreetly in your pocket, wear them on a cord around your neck, or hang them over the rearview mirror of your car. If you have a desk job, try keeping one in a drawer that you use frequently.

The main thing is to keep your charm bag in a place where you'll see it on a daily basis. If you find, after some time has gone by, that you're not really noticing it anymore, then move it to a new location where it will catch your attention again.

You can find small, inexpensive drawstring bags made of cotton, silk, or muslin at most craft stores, or order them online. Alternatively, you can make a charm "bundle" with a piece of scrap cloth gathered up at the corners and tied with a ribbon.

You will need:

- 1 small drawstring bag
- 3 small crystals of your choice
- ¼ cup dried flowers and/or dried herbs of your choice
- 1 small square of paper (about 1 inch by 1 inch)
- Pencil (or pen) and/or markers or crayons

- 1 tea light or votive candle

Instructions:

This charm bag should be as personalized as possible. Choose stones and herbs that have spiritual significance for you. If you're new to crystals and/or herbs, here are some suggestions, all of which have associations with spiritual strength and development:

Crystals: amethyst, blue calcite, kyanite, malachite, moonstone, quartz crystal.

Herbs: basil, cinnamon, dandelion, lavender, mug, sage.

Note: If you prefer to use potpourri instead of individual herbs, try to go with an all- natural blend, as synthetic fragrances tend to be disruptive to personal energy.

Light the candle as you hold your intention to create a powerful talisman that will keep you connected to your inner self throughout your day.

Take the piece of paper and draw a symbol on it that has meaning for you—perhaps a pentacle, a particular rune, a tree leaf, or any other image that resonates for you with magical energy. If you like, use markers or crayons to color in or around the symbol—feel free to infuse it with as much artistic power as you can!

Place the symbol next to the candle, being careful not to burn the paper.

Next, take a small pinch of the dried herbs or flowers and rub it between your palms for a few seconds. Then clap your hands together, allowing the crumbled herbs to fall away and sprinkle around your work area. (It's fun to let a few specks land in the candle flame, but not necessary).

Place the remaining herbs in the charm bag.

Take each crystal, one at a time, and hold it in your dominant hand.

Feel yourself sending your purest, strongest magical power into each stone, and then place it in the charm bag.

Finally, add the symbol to the bag, and pull the strings to close it.

Hold it in your hands, gaze into the candle flame, and say these words (or similar words of your own):

> *"As within, so without*
> *Let my connection to spirit never be in doubt*
> *As above, so below*
> *I bring this magic wherever I go"*

Place the charm bag next to the candle and leave it there until the candle burns all the way out on its own. It is now fully charged and ready to go!

NEXT STEPS

As you begin to incorporate the Craft more and more into your lifestyle, you may start considering making a formal commitment of some kind. In the next section, we'll examine the process of initiation into the Craft. We'll start with a look at some basic aspects of the coven experience, and then offer possible avenues for solitary practitioners.

Remember that there's no rush to enact a formal ritual to mark your relationship with this highly personal spiritual practiced. But if it feels right to you, it can be a wonderful milestone on your ongoing journey.

PART TWO

INITIATION AND SELF-DEDICATION

WHAT IS INITIATION?

For most people, the word "initiation" brings to mind a ritual or ceremony in which a person is admitted into a specific organization, usually of a secretive nature.

If your aim is to join a traditional coven, then this is an apt description. However, if you're a solitary Witch, the terminology for this important step along your path is a little less clear-cut.

This is because the conventional sense of *initiation*, particularly in the early days of the rise of modern Witchcraft, has involved the passing down of specific traditions from one Witch to another.

In this lineage system, would-be members of a coven will study under the mentorship of initiated, experienced members until they are knowledgeable and practiced enough to participate in coven rituals, and—most importantly—to commit themselves to spiritual fellowship with the group. Once these initiates have advanced enough along the path of their coven's tradition, they may eventually come to initiate new members.

Therefore, most members of traditional covens, especially those within the Wiccan community, hold the view that one cannot be initiated by anyone other than an already-initiated Witch.

Those who practice a solitary form of the Craft may study diligently from books and other resources, and may choose to enact a solitary ritual that acknowledges their decision to pursue this spiritual path, but because they are undertaking their learning and practice on their own, rather than through mentorship from an initiated Witch, they are not seen as being *initiated.*

Instead, the more widely-recognized term for a solitary Witch's formal entrance into the Craft is *self-dedication.* A ritual of self-dedication may resemble aspects of a coven initiation to varying degrees, but because solitary Witches can design and perform this ritual in any way they like, it is a fundamentally different experience.

Self-dedication happens strictly on your own terms. The commitment you're declaring in such a ritual is really to your inner self, to any deities you may incorporate into your practice, and to the divinity of the Universe as you understand it. It's not a commitment to any other person. It's not an entrance into a group of fellow practitioners. Therefore, according to traditionalists, it can't be an initiation.

Of course, there are counter-arguments to be made here. For one thing, the initiatory lineage of any given coven can't be traced back any further than the middle of the 20th century, when modern Wicca was developed. (There may be a small number of non-Wiccan covens that go back further, but if so, they are highly secretive and very unlikely to be openly recruiting new members.) This means that somewhere along the line, a Witch would have had to self-initiate.

And the same thing happens today in communities where new covens are formed without the assistance of an already-initiated leader—clearly, someone has to self-initiate in order to initiate the others.

So while everyone is entitled to their own perspective on the Craft, don't let those who follow a different set of rules determine how you describe your own personal ritual.

If you like the word "initiation," use it. In fact, you might even choose to view the word in light of its second definition: *the action of beginning something*, since when you self-initiate, you are truly setting your journey along the path into motion.

On the other hand, if "self-dedication" makes more sense to you, then go with it. After all, if you're a solitary Witch— especially if you're following an eclectic path— you can call your ritual anything you like.

For the purposes of the discussion below, the terms "self-initiation" and "self-dedication" are considered to be interchangeable.

But first, we'll take a closer look at the coven approach, for those who would like to know more about initiation in its "classic" form.

INITIATION IN TRADITIONAL COVENS

Traditionally, the act of initiation into a coven involves a highly ritualized ceremony.

In keeping with the traditions of secrecy regarding the Craft, the vast majority of covens do not share the details of their rituals with outsiders. That being said, there are some general characteristics that many coven processes have in common—and initiation is indeed a *process*, a series of steps leading to an experience of spiritual transformation that involves, but is not limited to, the moment of the rite itself.

First, there's a period of time in which the would-be initiate meets and spends time with the coven members, learning basic information about the coven's history and the tradition(s) they follow, and generally getting a sense for whether or not this particular group is a good fit.

This is a crucial undertaking, for both the individual and the coven. Unlike a circle, which is a more informal group of Witches who can rotate in and out as it suits their needs, a coven needs its members to be wholly committed to participating in rituals and contributing their energy on a consistent basis.

If you're initiating into a coven, you're asserting that you intend to stay—not necessarily for the rest of your natural life, but potentially so. You will also be forging intense bonds of friendship and spiritual fellowship that cannot be taken lightly. So you and your fellow potential coveners need to be sure not only that you'll get along well, but that you resonate harmoniously with each other on the deepest levels.

If at any point during this time period, you feel that something is "off" in any way, listen to your intuition! Don't be afraid to address any concerns or questions you may have about initiation or any other aspects of coven life. If you don't feel comfortable enough to discuss them, or if doing so doesn't resolve your concerns, then respectfully walk away. It may just not be meant to be, at least at this time.

If you do find a good fit and decide to begin the initiation process, you will then enter a period of study and mentorship with one or more experienced members of the coven.

The length of this process can vary widely, but most Wiccan covens observe the "year and a day" tradition at a minimum. During this time, you'll be immersing yourself in the beliefs and practices followed by the coven, and, depending on the coven's degree of eclecticism, possibly engaging in your own explorations of the mysteries of the Craft as well.

As a result, you will gradually (and sometimes, seemingly suddenly) find yourself changing from the inside out. Your perceptions of the world will be shifting as you awaken to the unseen energies of the Universe. Your relationship with the deities of your chosen path will unfold and strengthen.

You may also experience uncomfortable shifts in your relationships with others in your life, as you become less interested in the distractions of the modern world and focus your energy on your spiritual development.

Don't be concerned about this—those in your life who are meant to stay in your life will eventually adjust. In the meantime, understand this period of discomfort or disharmony as a natural part of the process. While it's true that initiation is all about new beginnings, it also involves an ending of your old way of life. A certain amount of separation from your former mode of existence—whether it's giving up a toxic TV habit or letting go of an unhealthy friendship—is to be expected.

When you encounter self-doubt—and you most likely will—simply calm your mind, allow yourself to sit with the doubt until you can see it clearly, and let it go. You will eventually come back to your center and remember that you're honoring your truest self by following this path.

As the date of your initiation draws near, you will likely be instructed on how to make your specific preparations for the rite. Again, this will vary widely, but the process usually involves some kind of cleansing or purification ritual, which may be in the form of a bath or shower, or a more symbolic cleansing. Meditation in the days and/or hours before the ceremony is another key component, as you will want to have a clear, calm, and focused mind going into the experience.

Depending on the coven's traditions, the ritual itself may involve the full coven or just a few members, and may be very elaborate or quite simple. Regardless of the specific form it takes, the focus of the ritual will be on acknowledging your commitment to the path of the Craft the coven follows, the deities the coven worships, and spiritual fellowship with the coven members themselves. This declaration is then honored by the coven by welcoming you into the fold, usually accompanied by a celebration of some kind.

While you may not know much about the details prior to the actual event, you should have a general sense of what will transpire.

For example, in some Wiccan covens, initiates are naked (also known as "skyclad") and blindfolded, with arms lightly bound behind them. (The coven members may or may not be skyclad.) This is to solidify the bonds of love and trust between the initiate and the coven, as well as the initiate and the deities. This tradition goes back to the beginnings of Gardnerian Wicca and is not practiced universally, but it's common enough to warrant mentioning here.

If the coven you're joining practices skyclad, you should be aware of this ahead of time, and you should be very comfortable and sure of the people you are working with. Ritual nudity has, unfortunately, attracted sexual predators to the Craft. Abuse of the practice isn't a common occurrence, and if you've been listening to your intuition throughout your journey with the coven, then it's highly unlikely that any unsavory energy would go undetected for this long.

Nonetheless, it's important to look out for yourself. If at any point in the proceedings you feel threatened or unsafe, or if anyone tells you to do anything you're uncomfortable doing, then don't be afraid to walk away right then and there. You can still honor what you've learned from this experience, and trust the Universe to connect you with the right group of people when it's the right time to do so.

Once you're initiated, you will be responsible for keeping your commitments to the coven—to show up for rituals and other meetings, to honor any vows of secrecy, and to be part of the support system that coven membership offers. Depending on the coven you belong to, there may be also further opportunities for structured advancement in your studies, in the form of a degree system.

This is usually found in traditional Wiccan covens, though some non-Wiccan forms of the Craft also observe some kind of tiered system, whether they use the word "degree" or different terminology. Witches who choose to pursue their studies formally in this way will usually go through additional initiation rituals to mark their achievements, and in many cases this is required for any Witch who wishes to initiate others.

Of course, in the widely diverse world of the Craft, there also are plenty of covens that operate without any kind of hierarchy, so if you have a strong preference one way or the other, this is definitely something to consider before beginning your initiation process.

It should be clear by now that initiation into a coven is not something to be taken lightly. You are entering into very strong emotional and spiritual bonds with the individuals in this group, so you need to be extremely compatible with them.

In fact, some Witches have likened initiation to marriage, and many people find that they are closer their fellow coveners than they are to their own family. So don't ever join a coven just because you want to belong to a group of Witches, or you are likely to regret your choice.

Indeed, it's definitely better to practice on your own than to become bound to a situation that is anything less than joyful, caring, and fulfilling.

If your desire is truly to belong to a coven, but the right opportunity hasn't yet come your way, take that as a signal from the Universe that it just isn't time yet. In the meantime, you can find other ways to connect with like-minded souls, such as through an informal Witches' circle or even an online community. You can also still devote yourself to studying the Craft on your own, and self-initiate/self-dedicate whenever it feels right to you.

If and when you do end up finding (or even forming) your ideal coven, you can then undergo a new initiation, if you choose. But whatever the case, know that you do not need another person to initiate you in order for you to "become" a Witch, no matter what anyone says.

INITIATION IN SOLITARY PRACTICE

Although solitary initiation, or self-dedication, is a very different experience from that of a coven initiation, there are still important parallels on the journey to this milestone on your path.

First, of course, is the work of really getting a feel for the Craft—exploring possible avenues in terms of established traditions, getting a sense for what resonates with you and what doesn't, etc.

But while you may choose to communicate and even spend time with people who share your interests during this time (and you may even already have friends who do), ultimately you're still sorting out for yourself what you want your relationship with the Craft to feel like, without also having to determine whether you want to join forces with others in an official way.

You will also, no doubt, experience internal shifts that end up causing some (or even all) of your interpersonal relationships to change, as well as any elements of your lifestyle that may be interfering with your connection to your inner self and your pursuit of the Craft.

There is also some overlap in terms of preparing for the ritual, namely meditation and cleansing or purification—or at least, it's highly recommended that you incorporate these elements.

But such recommendations are just that—there is no real prescribed path, no set of absolute instructions, no one to show you exactly what to do, and no one to do it but you.

This is the chief difference in a solitary initiation, and for many Witches, it's the chief appeal of solitary practice in general. However, others find the lack of established protocol daunting, wishing instead to be led by more experienced practitioners.

Luckily, there are plenty of ways to approach self-dedication with a reasonable amount of structure, if that's your preference. You can find books and online resources that will offer you a well-defined path, from actual interactive classes to recommended book lists, and more.

If you're looking to follow a specific, established practice rather than building your own eclectic form, you can find some good contemporary models, such as Raymond Buckland's *Complete Book of Witchcraft*, or

Scott Cunningham's *Wicca: A Guide for the Solitary Practitioner.*

Both of these classic books cover a wide range of elements of the Craft and plenty of practical information, including detailed rituals for self-dedication that you can follow to the letter, if you wish.

And while it's true that you cannot really access the kind of information found only in lineage-based, oath-bound coven traditions, such as Gardnerian Wicca, the practices outlined in these resources are rooted in various branches of these earlier forms, including Gardnerian and Alexandrian Wicca.

If you're seeking a decidedly non-Wiccan path, there are also established traditions such as Italian-based Stregheria, Cochrane's Craft, and contemporary Sabbatic Craft. You can also explore the Feri tradition, an older form that does require study with an initiate to truly learn the heart of it, but does not require coven participation.

If you're more eclectically inclined, you will most likely want to borrow from more than one tradition as you develop your practice, rather than adopting a single form or following a specific course. But you can still set yourself a course of study to follow as you work your way toward the point where you feel ready for initiation. Many solitaries find the year-and-a-day tradition very useful as a means of establishing some structure to their endeavor.

You can also "assign" yourself a certain amount of reading per week, organize your studies around specific topics such as the Wheel of the Year, and/or read all the books written by a particular author before moving on to a new one. Then again, you may want to be more free-wheeling and unmethodical about your study, following your inner guide from moment to moment until you're thoroughly inspired to perform your self-dedication.

When it comes to the ritual itself, if you haven't found one you want to follow in any of the sources you've consulted, then you will need to design your own. You may want to piece one together from various sources, possibly including some details from your own inspiration. Or, you might invent one entirely from scratch.

Below is an example "template" ritual that follows a fairly standard form, yet allows for you to tailor it to suit your individual path.

A RITUAL FOR SELF-INITIATION/ SELF-DEDICATION

This ritual is designed for the solitary practitioner of a non-specific form of Witchcraft. You can follow the instructions below to the letter, or you can use it as a template for creating your own self-dedication ritual.

Because not all Witches recognize a Goddess and/or God, the language used to address and describe "the powers that be" is intentionally open-ended.

Those wishing to acknowledge or emphasize their deities can tailor the wording to suit this purpose. For example, you may be dedicating yourself to "the gods" rather than "the path."

This is a highly personal undertaking, so spend some time thinking about how you want to verbalize your commitment.

THE PREPARATION

Here are a few things for you to consider prior to the self-initiation.

Choose a Date

You might find yourself inspired to enact your self-dedication immediately, but it's best to plan ahead and honor the process of preparing for it, especially if you want it to have a lasting impact.

Choose a date that has some significance for you, either personally or in terms of what's happening in the cosmos. A new moon is an ideal time, but you might also wish to coordinate it with a solstice, or with the beginning of a new astrological sign.

Whatever you decide, give yourself at least a week ahead of time to prepare.

Choose a Place

If you can find an outdoor location in a natural setting where you can be sure you won't be disturbed, this is ideal—even if it's just your backyard. But don't think for a minute that you can't have an equally powerful experience indoors—what matters is that you are alone and in quiet surroundings.

Perhaps you already have a sacred space and/or an altar established in your home—if so, this is a perfect place. If not, consider creating a sacred space for yourself as a first step in your preparations.

You will then be able to return to this space again and again for rituals and spellwork.

Prepare Your Inner Self

For at least one week leading up to the date of your ritual, spend at least a few minutes every day in meditation, preferably at the same time each day.

After you come out of meditation, take a few moments to contemplate your spiritual aspirations. Why are you choosing to formally dedicate yourself to the Craft? What is it, exactly, that you want to communicate to the Universe and/or your deities through the enactment of this ritual? And how do you imagine you will feel afterward?

Take some time to visualize and then practice *feeling* your connection to the magical energies of the Divine.

Do some free writing about your experiences thus far—learning about the Craft, discovering your path, exploring magic, etc.—and about what you would like to see unfold in the future.

As you write, you may come up with some words and phrases that you can use in your ritual, in addition to or instead of the words offered below.

Gather Your Tools

If your ritual takes place inside, you'll need the following:

- 6 tea lights (in holders)
- 1 white pillar candle
- Small bowl of salt or soil
- Anointing oil. This can be a purchased blend, or a homemade blend of essential oil and carrier oil, such as almond or olive oil. (Do not use essential oils directly on skin—mix them with a carrier oil first.) Sandalwood, frankincense, and myrrh are often used for initiation rites, but use a scent that is pleasing to you. And if you don't have access to essential oils, you can simply use olive oil on its own.
- Paper and pen/pencil for writing down your ritual words. (This is optional, but it's recommended to either have this memorized, or have it with you on paper so you don't scatter mental energy trying to remember what to say.)

If you're outside, you don't need the salt or soil, and depending on location and weather conditions, you may want to scale down on the candles. Just one is fine, but if even this isn't possible, you can use an upturned flashlight, or make the shape of a flame with your palms pressed together, fingers pointing to the sky.

A note on clothing: many Witches perform their self-dedication skyclad. If this is possible and you're comfortable with it, go for it. If you have ritual robes, that can be a powerful alternative.

Really, you should wear whatever feels right to you, but do make sure you choose something to wear that marks this occasion somehow. In other words, don't self-dedicate wearing what you wore to work or school that day.

And if at all possible, go barefoot—especially if you're inside.

THE RITUAL

Just before you're ready to begin, take a ritual cleansing bath (or shower) with sea salt. (You can salt a washcloth for use in the shower.)

Visualize the mundane details of your day dissolving, and imagine that you're clearing away any unwanted aspects of your old life, before you discovered your new path.

Afterward, sit in meditation for 5 to 10 minutes to clear your mind. Take some long, slow deep breaths to ground and center yourself.

When you're ready, arrange the tea lights in a circle around you and place the pillar candle in front of you. Sprinkle the salt or soil onto the floor within the circle. Light the tea lights, then stand with your feet in the salt or earth. Take another few deep breaths.

Now it's time to announce your intention formally to the Universe. You can say the following words, or words of your own:

"I stand upon the Earth in this time, in this place, to declare my dedication to my path of the Craft. I now release any doubt, old fears, old limiting beliefs, and any and all resistance to fully embracing this new life."

Now, anoint yourself with the oil, starting with the pulse points of your wrists and neck, then the center of your brow, and finally your heart. (Some traditions go further and anoint eyelids, lips, hands, genitals, and the soles of the feet—do what seems right for you.)

Be very present for this, really focusing on the feel of the oil on your skin—this is the action that symbolizes the joining of your physical self with the non-physical energy of the Universe.

When you're finished, say the following words, or words of your own:

"I welcome my sacred connection to the Earth,
and give thanks for the life-sustaining
gifts of her abundance.
I dedicate myself to the wisdom of the Craft,
and to continued growth and learning.
I welcome constant communion with the divine.
I embrace the change I am making in this time and place.
I welcome this initiation into the
mysteries of the Divine All.
I rejoice in my path."

To seal your dedication, light the pillar candle. Close with these (or your own) words:

"From now on, I walk my path with purpose,
joyfully aware of my divine connection to All That Is."

Sit still for several moments and bask in the glow of the energetic connection you have just created.

If you're outdoors, listen for bird calls, wind stirring the trees, or any other signals that the natural world is responding to your energy. If you're indoors, gaze softly at the candle flame and watch how it dances in celebration of your actions.

After your ritual, avoid going straight into any mundane activity for the rest of the day (such as cleaning, watching TV or checking social media). Do something special to celebrate, instead.

And from now on, be intentionally open to a new level of connection with the spirit world. You have sent forth a very powerful intention, and that divine love will be returned to you in new and surprising ways.

MOVING FORWARD

As you can see, initiation can take many forms, and is truly a process rather than just a single event. It can be seen as a beginning, but it can also be seen as an honoring of the progress you've made along your path thus far, even as you are stepping into new territory.

If you've prepared yourself adequately and taken the ritual seriously, by being truly present to it and trusting your own process, then you will very likely feel that a change has taken place. Joyous, excited, invigorated, renewed—these are just a few of the words Witches have used to describe their state of mind in the days following their initiation/dedication. But what happens now?

If you've initiated into a coven, you'll most likely be receiving and assimilating new knowledge, and participating in group ritual and magic on a new level. But if you're solitary, your life may not seem a whole lot different—at least, not in any obvious ways.

Don't be alarmed if this is the case. The truth is that, coven or no coven, an initiation ritual is not going to suddenly transform you into a full-time Witch all by itself.

It's still, and always will be, a process. You will still be responsible for your own continued learning and growth, and your own level of participation in active communion with the deities and/or the force(s) of energy you work with. As a solitary, it will still be up to you to celebrate the full moon, to work a spell, to meditate, and to explore new ways of approaching ritual and magic.

If you can remember back to Part One, we discussed the challenges faced by the aspiring Witch—one of the biggest being the difficulty of finding the time to immerse yourself in a "*witchy*" lifestyle. Many of us *want* to practice Witchcraft daily, but life gets in the way.

The act of initiation can bring in powerful inspiration for continuing your practice of the Craft. But acting on that inspiration will still be your decision, with each step of your long and winding path.

Part Three was created for anyone looking to deepen their involvement with the Craft, by making it part of your daily routines. In it, we'll explore some ideas and practices that, over time, can deeply enrich your day to day life as a Witch, expand your capacity to attract magical manifestations, and navigate your way through challenging times.

You might view these offerings as inspiration for your next steps in the post-initiation life. However, this next section is intended to be just as useful for those who have not yet reached this milestone, and even for those who do not choose to make initiation a goal. You can think of it as a collection of "tips for the trail," no matter where you are on yours!

PART THREE
GUIDEPOSTS

A WAY OF LIFE

This guide began with the metaphor of "the path" to describe the process of discovering, learning about, and developing a practice of Witchcraft.

Within this metaphor, the act of initiation is seen as a highly significant point, or milestone, that celebrates your decision to commit to moving forward on your path, whether it be through an established Craft tradition or your own individualized form.

But no matter how your process unfolds, this path is ideally experienced as a way of life, rather than merely as a series of rituals marking the phases of the moon and the journey of the sun around the Earth.

You can go through the motions and follow all the spells and rites you find in your favorite books, but this won't necessarily cause your spiritual self—your delightful *witchiness*—to come through for you in an authentic, deeply felt way.

Ultimately, what we might call "spiritual satisfaction" occurs through being awake and aware on your path as much as possible. Just as you wouldn't spend a nature hike staring only at the ground just ahead of your feet, you don't want to miss the sights and sounds, the beautiful vistas and the quiet, sacred moments of a life in the Craft.

And the more you are available to perceive and allow these moments, the more they will occur, until eventually you are feeling the magical undercurrents of the world around you far more often than not.

This state of being can be achieved by developing new habits of perception that put you more in touch with your sixth sense more of the time, developing and strengthening your inner knowing and opening you up to experiencing more evidence of the inherent magic of the Universe.

There are countless avenues toward this pursuit, which include meditation, divination, journaling, petitioning your deities, spirit guides, or any other energies you work with for guidance, and observing and appreciating the positive manifestations—both material and immaterial—of your practice.

It's also rewarding to develop and maintain your receptivity to messages from the unseen world, which will igate your way along your path. The onstantly providing signs and signals to you day experience, from subtle affirmations that you're on the right track, to gentle (or not so gentle) warnings to reconsider your current course of action. Depending on your level of receptivity, you may or may not recognize these moments for what they are—but with practice, you definitely will.

Depending on your beliefs, you may experience these messages as being from specific spirit guides, ancestors, elemental energies, or deities—and there can be different messages from different sources—or you might just perceive them to be from "the Universe."

We'll use this last term below for the sake of simplicity, as we explore a few ways in which you can discover the magic of seemingly ordinary moments. These practices do not belong strictly to the realm of Witchcraft, but they share plenty of territory, and they inform the practice of many a Witch.

Like the study and practice of Tarot, runes, and other traditional forms of divination, these are methods of inviting communication from the spirit world. But unlike those active modes, which you can initiate with a question whenever you want to, these are more passive—or receptive—in that your only role is simply to observe and be open.

ANIMAL MESSENGERS

In the ancient world, animals were widely understood to have spirits, or souls, of their own. In myths and stories from around the globe, animals have interacted with human beings, and have even been responsible for the actual creation of the Universe.

In these traditions, animals were not subordinate to humans, but equals. Humans derived benefit from their association with animals, not only in the form of food, clothing, and other goods made from their bodies, but in the form of spiritual protection and wisdom as well.

Many cultures had specific "clan animals" or "totems" to represent distinct groups within their societies, as well as individual animal allies or helpers, variously known as spirit animals, power animals, or totem animals. These relationships between animals and humans are found in Norse, Celtic, and Native American traditions, among many others, and are still honored in living shamanic cultures today.

To some extent, the concept of spirit animals has spread to modern Witchcraft. Of course, the lore of the Craft in Western Europe is full of tales of animal "familiars," but much of it is either Christianized, fancifully exaggerated, or both, so it's hard to know what relationships between Witches and familiars truly entailed.

Still, many Witches today work with animals in both physical and spiritual form. Many deities from the ancient pantheons have long been associated with specific animals, and Witches who work with these deities may choose to use images of the deity's animal in ritual or spellwork.

In some forms of magic, the essence, or spirit of an animal, such as the wolf, the bear, or the eagle can be called upon to aid or guide the work. And plenty of Witches share their homes with cats, birds, and other companion animals who are part of their magical lives.

In recent decades, many Witches have adopted the shamanic belief that everyone has specific spirit animals. It's said that a few of these stay with us from birth to death, but others will come and go from our lives as our circumstances change. Whether or not you incorporate this belief into your practice, it's definitely worth paying attention to animal symbolism as a means of spiritual messaging.

If you study their behavior, you'll find that animals have useful lessons to offer people regarding how to live successfully on Earth. So if a particular animal keeps popping up into your awareness, it's likely that that animal has some advice to offer you.

For example, squirrels are thought to bring a message of the importance of balancing work and play. Alternatively, they may be signaling that you need to be sure your material bases are covered. The spider is a reminder of the virtues of patience and persistence, as well as the importance of viewing a situation from every angle.

Animals can also serve as omens, offering information about a present or future situation. The crow, long associated with warnings of death, can also appear to those on the spiritual path on the eve of some kind of personal transformation. The deer can point to an upcoming new adventure and let you know that you are being gently encouraged to take advantage of it.

Furthermore, your deceased loved ones in the spirit world can, and often do, come to you in the form of animals. This happens most often with birds, butterflies, and other brightly-colored animals that stay in your presence for just a short time. So if you've ever "felt" the presence of someone on the other side when a particular animal is around, you can bet that you received a visit!

If you're not already tapped into the magical realm of animal communication, start being more aware of how animals figure into your experience. This includes animals who literally cross your path in your daily life, as well as those you encounter in dreams and in other imagery.

There is a wealth of information in books and online sources you can turn to for interpretations of these animal communications, so you can always look up any animal that catches your attention. Of course, not every sighting of an animal is necessarily significant—as they say, sometimes a bird is just a bird. But if a particular animal starts showing up in your life repeatedly, consider the possibility that it's trying to tell you something.

Sometimes it will be quite obvious that there's a message, such as when a wild animal "randomly" enters your house, or when you're having recurring dreams about the same animal. But often it can be subtle.

Perhaps you keep seeing giraffes in various unrelated posts on social media, and then a birthday card arrives in the mail with a giraffe on the cover. Or maybe you keep seeing robins whenever you're worrying about a particular problem in your life.

These moments can be seen as invitations to pause, take a step back, and seek a new perspective on whatever has been going on in your life. They could also be signals to stay open to new developments that are just around the corner.

Take a moment to communicate with the spirit energy of any animal that crosses your path in a distinctive way. Thank it for visiting you, and do some research to find out more specifically what it has to say to you. As you make a deliberate practice of these observations, you will find that

the Universe responds by sending you even more
messages from the animal kingdom.

"SCRYING" IN NATURE

The term "scrying" usually refers to the art of seeing images in a reflective surface, for the purposes of divination.

Like much of magic, scrying is a skill that takes practice—very few beginners are able to gaze into a crystal ball and instantly get results. It's also harder than other forms of divination, such as Tarot cards or runes, because there's no system of specific images and associated meanings to work with.

Instead, what the scryer sees in the crystal, mirror, or bowl of water could literally be *anything*, and only the scryer can interpret the images and symbols, which makes it a very personal and individualized process.

But whether or not you have interest or ability in the art of scrying itself, this concept can be used to open up a wealth of opportunities to interact with the magical energy of the natural world. Nature offers countless "surfaces" for seeing images in, and not just glassy lakes, ponds and puddles. You can receive stunning visual messages from gazing with a soft focus at flames, clouds, trees, and just about anything else you see.

Looking at nature in this way helps you to exercise a weaker intuitive "muscle," as you rely exclusively on your visual perception, with no need for language—and this is particularly good for people with highly analytical and/or verbal minds.

What you see when you practice this subtle art may be reflecting something about your inner process or present circumstances, but it may also just be about connecting with the divine mystery, allowing your spirit to engage in some much-needed "play time."

No matter where or how you grew up, you almost certainly spent time as a child watching the clouds for shapes and faces as they floated by. This is perhaps the easiest and most common form of "nature-scrying," and was practiced by our ancestors probably since the dawn of humanity.

While clouds of any type or size can create a good canvas in any kind of weather, there's something particularly magical about large, thick clouds with a lot of color variation due to storms or sunlight, as these can produce the most complex and stunning images.

Fast-moving clouds are also wonderful for their ability to keep changing "the scene" as they sail by! In fact, in the right circumstances, the sky can seem to be putting on a lively and action-packed drama with multiple characters and stories.

If you abandoned the practice of cloud-watching after you left childhood, now is a good time to pick it back up. The next time you find yourself with 10 or 15 minutes free on a good cloud-watching day, go outside and just stare up at the sky.

Let go of any current worries and distractions and let your focus soften as the clouds pass over you. What shapes and/or images can you see? How are the edges of the clouds interacting with each other? Don't try to force any images to become recognizable to you as anything in particular. Simply watch the show and see what arises.

Clouds may seem to be among the most obvious natural scrying tools, but trees also offer excellent "canvases," particularly in the summer months when they are fully fleshed out with leaves. If you soften your gaze when looking at them, you'll likely find that all kinds of faces pop out— among the leaves as well as on trunks and branches.

Many people fondly refer to these faces as "the faeries," while others see them as representations of the Goddess and God. Plenty of other shapes can also appear, most often those of animals.

As with cloud-watching, windy days can be particularly good for scrying among leafy trees, since the images can change rapidly with the wind's movement. But it isn't strictly necessary for there to be leaves on the trees, nor does it have to be daytime—the stark contrast of bare branches against the moonlit sky can also create fantastic magical imagery.

So next time you're blessed to have one or more trees in your view, start taking notice of what you can see in the leaves, branches, and trunks. If there are trees visible from a window where you live, pay attention to the images that arise at various times of the day and the year.

Stones are another great source of naturally-occurring imagery. Whether you're gazing at large boulders in a natural setting, or examining small rocks you've picked up along hikes, you can find plenty of images in the lines and color variations found in common stones.

Many stones—and seashells for that matter—from certain geological areas contain tiny fossils of organisms millions of years old. These delightful images can be thought of as ancient "postcards" from past eras!

One nice aspect of these more permanent works of art is that you can look at them again and again, unlike the more fleeting images you see in clouds and trees. But temporary canvases can be just as compelling, whether they be in the sky or on the ground—such as the patterns on a shoreline made from incoming waves, or tracks made by animals in the snow.

And let's not forget the classic and perhaps most magical scrying source known to humans—fire! Whether it's a boisterous bonfire or the quiet flame of a single flickering candle, the imagery found within fire can be truly mesmerizing.

Really, once you get into the habit of viewing so much of the world in this way, you can start seeing shapes and faces in just about anything that has variations in lines and/or coloring, whether it's a natural object or not.

For example, some Witches like to examine the melted wax of spent candles for messages about the outcome of their spellwork. You can even see images in melting butter or oil in a skillet with the right perceptual awareness!

The psychological term for this ability is "pareidolia," which is usually defined as a tendency to interpret something known or familiar from a stimulus where it doesn't actually exist. (This is what explains the sometimes widely-publicized phenomena of people seeing the face of Jesus or Mary in a piece of toast.) Some of these images, like the "man on the Moon," can be perceived by whole populations, while others are only recognizable to one person.

But while scientists may only be interested in the brain functions involved in this process, Witches and other intuitives know that there's something larger going on. It could be argued that the Universe is just one giant tapestry of imagery and message, always communicating, and always alive to new interpretations from new recipients of the information it offers.

As you practice seeing in this way, it's possible that you'll perceive images that seem to indicate negativity, such as unsmiling or even seemingly-menacing faces in a cloud or the trunk of a tree.

Don't get swept up in interpreting these visions from a place of fear. There could be many reasons for what you perceive as "negative" messaging.

For example, you may be picking up a reflection of a feeling within yourself, such as the dread of an upcoming exam or sadness after an argument with a friend. You might also simply be misunderstanding the energy of the image due to cultural conditioning.

Most of us have been trained to see a smile as the only real positive facial expression, and may assume that any other type of expression indicates unhappiness or negativity. But if you look at artistic representations of deities, spirits, faeries, or other manifestations of the invisible world—particularly those from pre-modern times—you will often see unsmiling faces on these benevolent beings. So don't automatically assume that a less-than-joyous image is an "ill omen."

In fact, this practice is just as much an exercise in perception as a way of receiving specific information. It's about training your mind to look past the ordinary, expected view of the objects in your world, and opening your awareness to the subtle, less-seen aspects of reality.

As you develop this practice over time, you may find that there is a pattern of correspondence between what you see and what you're experiencing in your life, but even then, not every image you see in a cloud or a stone is going to be a significant communication meant just for you. Sometimes a face is just a face. The point is that you're strengthening your connection to the Universe by being receptive to its subtle beauty.

THE MAGIC
OF NUMBERS

Have you ever had times in your life when you seem to "randomly" look at the clock at the same time every day? Or times when the same number keeps popping up in many different ways in a short span of time?

Maybe you see the same pattern of numbers repeatedly, such as sequential sets (123, 987, etc.) or triple digits (444, 222, etc.) Or perhaps you keep coming across numbers that are personally significant to you—such as the digits of your birthday, or the address of your childhood home.

Whatever the case, if specific numbers are showing up in your life in unusual or otherwise noticeable ways, then you can safely assume that the Universe is trying to tell you something.

Numerical messages can be delightful "puzzles" to work out. Even if you've never had much interest in numerology, the meanings of numbers on their own are worth investigating when particular numbers are getting your attention.

You don't need to delve into the various ways in which numerologists assign and interpret your personal numbers, which generally have to do with your date of birth and the letters of your name—although that information can be illuminating as well for those who are interested. Simply having a look into the ways in which the numbers themselves are interpreted can open up a new world of understanding about where you are in your present life circumstances, and/or what the Universe is nudging you to learn about yourself.

For example, the number 8 is said to symbolize abundance and success. The number 5 can point to unpredictability and action, while 6 often deals with matters of relationships. Double and triple digit numbers also carry significance. If you're seeing the number 17 over and over again, this can be a hint that you need to work to stay true to your core spiritual values. Repeated sightings of 111 is a signal that what you're currently focusing on is being manifested, so paying attention to your thoughts is important at this time.

The most common places people see recurring numbers are on digital clocks, license plates, phone numbers, advertisements, and other signage, but they can also show up in other ways. You may come across a number repeatedly as you're reading or flipping through channels on the television, or hear it mentioned aloud by people in conversation.

A number can manifest not just as a numeral, but in other ways as well. For example, on a nature hike, some people might attribute meaning to the number of birds in a small flock flying overhead, or the number of trees in a sacred grove. For others, passing four of the exact same type of vehicle in a row on the highway may have significance.

Of course, Witches have long understood that numbers are powerful. Plenty of spellwork makes use of numbers in various ways. For example, the number of crystals or candles called for is generally quite intentional, as is the number of times a phrase or gesture is repeated.

The number three is particularly significant in many Wiccan forms of the Craft, as is seen in the Threefold Law and the Triple Goddess. Thirteen, of course, is also powerful for many in the Craft, and some Witches also highly value the number seven, as it has quite a lot of significance in religious and spiritual traditions around the world.

As you develop your own practice, consider keeping the energetic power of numbers in your awareness. You can find plenty of information about numerical symbolism online and in print resources, from a variety of spiritual systems—the classical numerology of the Western Mystery Tradition is just one option.

You'll most likely find a few different possible interpretations depending on where you look, but your intuition will help you discern which meaning is relevant to you and your situation. And no matter where you look for help in deciphering the message, once a number gets your attention and you begin exploring its significance, you'll find it popping up with even more frequency.

Keep in mind, of course, that just as with any other aspect of tuning into Universal messages, it's possible to go overboard, so beware of becoming obsessed with numbers! You can definitely become unnecessarily distracted if you're looking for a "sign" in every single number you come across in your daily life.

But if you've never given much thought to numbers before, it's worth starting to acquaint yourself with these timeless symbols, since they provide so many opportunities for the Universe to support you on your path.

READING THE SIGNS

There are infinite ways in which the mysterious energies of the unseen world can show up in your life.

It may happen in the form of psychic connections, such as when you're thinking of a friend or relative who then suddenly calls you out of the blue. Often it occurs as a series of seeming coincidences—or what others might call synchronicity or serendipity.

For example, you may hear a song on the radio with lyrics that perfectly describe your present circumstances in an eerie way. Or perhaps a specific book title or movie is mentioned in several different, unrelated conversations throughout your day.

Although these occurrences happen to everyone, they seem to be more pronounced and interesting for those who find themselves drawn to the Craft. However, being a Witch doesn't automatically make you more adept at understanding what, if anything, the messages are supposed to mean.

So how *do* you know whether something is a "sign," or just an interesting or odd coincidence? When is a bird just a bird?

This can be challenging to discern, since each person has a unique, individual relationship with the Universe and no two people experience these messages in the same way. However, there are a few factors to consider when you find yourself unsure about whether you're on the receiving end of divine communication.

First and foremost, check in with your gut.

Are you truly *feeling* a sense of significance around this event, or is it more like simple amusement? If you have a strong intuitive sense that something more is going on here, than you're probably correct. But if that intuitive "tug" isn't really present, then there's no need to give the occurrence further thought.

Another aspect to consider is the frequency and form of the occurrence. For example, hearing the same song on the radio repeatedly throughout the day is hardly unusual if it's a popular song in heavy rotation. But hearing a much lesser-known song a few times may be another story, particularly if you're hearing it in different and unexpected places.

Another example might be a specific phrase in a book that catches your attention, then later turns up in an unrelated conversation with a friend, and later still in a commercial. In other words, coincidences with a high degree of both frequency and improbability can generally be assumed to be more than just coincidence.

For most of us, the ability to identify and interpret messages from the spirit world comes gradually, with practice. Unless you were born with highly developed psychic gifts, this will often feel like guesswork, at least in the beginning.

But it's well worth the effort to keep at it, as you'll be developing two important and related elements of your experience along your path: a stronger connection to your intuition, and a personalized "vocabulary" through which you can receive information from the Universe, which may include animal visits, visions in the trees, numerological messages, and/or other mysterious events.

You'll truly be able to recognize and affirm those magical moments when the spirit world is giving you, and only you, a warm wink and a nod.

A WITCH'S JOURNAL—
KEEPING MAGICAL
RECORDS

If you're reading this guide, you have most likely already experienced plenty of interesting, and even exhilarating moments of magic in your life—moments when you've known that you're exactly where you're supposed to be, when you're sure that some unseen force is trying to tell you something, when evidence of a successful spell manifests, or when you've witnessed something that could only be explained as a "miracle."

While nearly everyone has had an experience or two like this at some point in their lives that they never forget, there are actually plenty of magical moments happening all around us that can easily go unnoticed—or briefly registered and then were forgotten.

Letting these occurrences slide under the radar of your awareness, however relatively insignificant they may seem, is like wasting perfectly good evidence of your magical connection to the Universe. Then, during those tough days or weeks that feel decidedly "unmagical" due to difficult circumstances, you may begin to have doubts about your belief in magic and/or the Craft. This is a common challenge for aspiring Witches who haven't yet had enough success in magic to keep the flame of their beliefs alive through the more difficult times.

Keeping a written record of your magical moments is a sure-fire way to keep yourself aligned with your path. When you have written evidence of your prior experience, you can use it to silence those negative thought forms that try to dissuade you from your beliefs.

It can be incredibly easy to forget even our most astounding encounters with the spirit world once a stubborn obstacle is staring us straight in the face, but if we've written them down, we can come back to those moments whenever we need a reminder that we really are being supported every step of the way.

What's more, the act of writing about magical moments automatically gives our memory of them more energy—in essence, creating positive thought forms that can be strengthened again every time we read back over what we've written.

And because like attracts like, the more we reinforce our thoughts and feelings around these positive encounters, the more magical moments we're inviting into our lives.

So what constitutes a "magical moment," exactly? What should you be writing down?

The answer varies from person to person, of course, but a general rule of thumb is anything that strikes you as out of the ordinary—an occurrence, however brief or fleeting, that seems to rise above the level of your mundane existence in order to get your attention.

This can include any of the "messaging systems" discussed above, such as interesting or unusual animal sightings, particularly striking images you may have noticed in a cloud or a clear puddle of water, or particular numbers showing up again and again throughout your day or your week.

Any other synchronicities or incidents that seem too strange to chalk up to "coincidence" should also be noted, as well as any significant dreams that you can recall. (Speaking of dreams, it's recommended that you write about your dreams as soon as you can, since the details can often be lost even minutes after you wake up.)

You may be quite unclear as to what any of these occurrences are supposed to "mean" to you as they're happening. This is fine—in fact, it's all the more reason to record them! You may very likely understand, after a few days or weeks have passed, what a particular message or set of messages is indicating.

In fact, the practice of recording and then revisiting these signs can really help you gain an appreciation for what is often called "divine timing." Sometimes, you are being tipped off to unfolding events in advance of their actual manifestation, because the messaging, however unclear it may seem, helps keep you alert enough to avoid being caught off-guard by the unexpected.

Furthermore, over time this practice can help you get a better sense of when "a bird is just a bird," because your intuition will get more finely tuned as you repeatedly ask yourself whether or not a particular occurrence really qualifies for you as a "magical moment."

In addition to the more mysterious signs and signals, be sure to record happy surprises, gifts, blessings—anything that stimulates or reinforces a positive view of your current circumstances is worth appreciating through writing!

It's also crucial to acknowledge any occurrence that can be seen as a manifestation of specific spellwork, even if it doesn't quite seem to hit the target you were aiming for. For example, if you've recently worked a money spell and then start finding coins on the ground or unexpected small bills in the pocket of a coat you haven't worn in awhile, record it—it's a start!

Keeping track of the results of your magic is an excellent way to learn which spells and methods work best for you. You might also want to write down the results of any divination sessions you participate in, such as Tarot readings, as these potentially handy details can often be difficult to recall later on.

How and where you keep your "magical records" is up to you. You might keep a journal specifically for this purpose—a "diary" of your experiences along your path. Or, if you keep a book of shadows, you could jot down the most significant occurrences there—particularly results of spellwork. Depending on your relationship with technology, you might even keep your records electronically—though many Witches would argue for the old-fashioned pen and paper method, as the physical act of handwriting is thought to reinforce the positive energy of recording the evidence of magic.

But no matter how you go about it, try to make it a consistent practice, and be sure to review what you've written from time to time—particularly when life seems to be short on magic. You'll be amazed at how reassuring it is to see the evidence to the contrary.

PARTING THOUGHTS

Whether you are actively working toward the milestone of initiation, or have already had this experience, or even if you are just continuing to explore the Craft without plans to formally mark your journey, these practices can enrich your life along your path.

As you get into the habit of increasing your awareness of the subtle energetic currents of the unseen world, you will find magic even in the midst of your "humdrum" everyday existence. Over time, you will experience more and more of a seamless weaving of the spiritual and the mundane, rather than an "ordinary" life punctuated by magical moments.

This progression into deeper spiritual territory is really what initiation is all about—the ongoing process of discovery, allowing your relationship with spirit to evolve beyond your expectations. Embrace and enjoy it!

CONCLUSION

Hopefully, this guide has provided helpful advice for navigating the twists and turns of your journey into the wonderful realms of the Craft. Of course, as you know by now, when it comes to the question of where to go next, you are your ultimately your own guide.

But whether you pursue a traditional path to initiation into one or more forms of Witchcraft, or maintain a solitary practice of self-dedication, know that there will always be more to discover.

Even if you end up being drawn to a different path altogether, honor yourself for having invested this time and energy to exploring the interests of your heart. And never doubt that everywhere you look, there is magic to be found.

On that note, I will say goodbye, as it's now time for you to continue on your path. I hope that this book has helped you to take a few more steps forward, and I wish you all the best on the rest of your journey. Keep reading and never stop learning, and who knows where your journey will take you!

Thank you one more time for reading.

Blessed Be.

SUGGESTIONS FOR FURTHER READING

Although this list is divided into Wiccan and non-Wiccan categories, there is often some overlap between the two.

Non-Wiccan sources may incorporate elements of Wicca into their practice, but do not identify their traditions as being Wiccan. Because there is less emphasis on initiation in many non-Wiccan forms of the Craft, books on this topic are a bit harder to come by.

Nonetheless, the sources listed below can help you broaden your horizons as they present many possible paths to initiation, self-dedication, and (most importantly) continued learning as you go forward with your journey. Please be aware that there are many more resources available in print and online in addition to these suggestions.

Happy reading!

Wicca

Raymond Buckland, *Buckland's Complete Book of Witchcraft* (1986)

Raymond Buckland, *Wicca for One: The Path of Solitary Witchcraft* (2004)

Scott Cunningham, *Wicca: A Guide for the Solitary Practitioner* (1989)

Janine DeMartini, *A Seeker's Journey and Initiation into Wicca* (2006)

Amethyst Treleven, *Seeker's Guide to Learning Wicca: Training to First Degree in The Northern Hemisphere* (2008)

Amethyst Treleven, *Seeker's Guide to Learning Wicca: Training to First Degree in The Southern Hemisphere* (2008)

<u>Traditional / Non-Wiccan Witchcraft</u>

Victor and Cora Anderson, *The Heart of the Initiate: Feri Lessons* (2012)

T. Thorn Coyle, *Make Magic of Your Life: Passion, Purpose, and the Power of Desire* (2013)

Christopher Penczak, *The Inner Temple of Witchcraft* (2002)

Christopher Penczak, *The Outer Temple of Witchcraft* (2012)

THREE FREE AUDIOBOOKS PROMOTION

Don't forget, you can now enjoy **three audiobooks completely free of charge** when you start a free 30-day trial with Audible.

If you're new to the Craft, *Wicca Starter Kit* contains three of Lisa's most popular books for beginning Wiccans. You can download it for free at:

www.wiccaliving.com/free-wiccan-audiobooks

Or, if you're wanting to expand your magical skills, check out *Spellbook Starter Kit,* with three collections of spellwork featuring the powerful energies of candles, colors, crystals, mineral stones, and magical herbs. Download over 150 spells for free at:

www.wiccaliving.com/free-spell-audiobooks

Members receive free audiobooks every month, as well as exclusive discounts. And, if you don't want to continue with Audible, just remember to cancel your membership. You won't be charged a cent, and you'll get to keep your books!

Happy listening!

MORE BOOKS BY
LISA CHAMBERLAIN

Wicca for Beginners: A Guide to Wiccan Beliefs, Rituals, Magic, and Witchcraft

Wicca Book of Spells: A Book of Shadows for Wiccans, Witches, and Other Practitioners of Magic

Wicca Herbal Magic: A Beginner's Guide to Practicing Wiccan Herbal Magic, with Simple Herb Spells

Wicca Book of Herbal Spells: A Book of Shadows for Wiccans, Witches, and Other Practitioners of Herbal Magic

Wicca Candle Magic: A Beginner's Guide to Practicing Wiccan Candle Magic, with Simple Candle Spells

Wicca Book of Candle Spells: A Book of Shadows for Wiccans, Witches, and Other Practitioners of Candle Magic

Wicca Crystal Magic: A Beginner's Guide to Practicing Wiccan Crystal Magic, with Simple Crystal Spells

Wicca Book of Crystal Spells: A Book of Shadows for Wiccans, Witches, and Other Practitioners of Crystal Magic

Tarot for Beginners: A Guide to Psychic Tarot Reading, Real Tarot Card Meanings, and Simple Tarot Spreads

Runes for Beginners: A Guide to Reading Runes in Divination, Rune Magic, and the Meaning of the Elder Futhark Runes

Wicca Moon Magic: A Wiccan's Guide and Grimoire for Working Magic with Lunar Energies

Wicca Wheel of the Year Magic: A Beginner's Guide to the Sabbats, with History, Symbolism, Celebration Ideas, and Dedicated Sabbat Spells

Wicca Kitchen Witchery: A Beginner's Guide to Magical Cooking, with Simple Spells and Recipes

Wicca Essential Oils Magic: A Beginner's Guide to Working with Magical Oils, with Simple Recipes and Spells

Wicca Elemental Magic: A Guide to the Elements, Witchcraft, and Magical Spells

Wicca Magical Deities: A Guide to the Wiccan God and Goddess, and Choosing a Deity to Work Magic With

Wicca Living a Magical Life: A Guide to Initiation and Navigating Your Journey in the Craft

Magic and the Law of Attraction: A Witch's Guide to the Magic of Intention, Raising Your Frequency, and Building Your Reality

Wicca Altar and Tools: A Beginner's Guide to Wiccan Altars, Tools for Spellwork, and Casting the Circle

Wicca Finding Your Path: A Beginner's Guide to Wiccan Traditions, Solitary Practitioners, Eclectic Witches, Covens, and Circles

Wicca Book of Shadows: A Beginner's Guide to Keeping Your Own Book of Shadows and the History of Grimoires

Modern Witchcraft and Magic for Beginners: A Guide to Traditional and Contemporary Paths, with Magical Techniques for the Beginner Witch

FREE GIFT REMINDER

Just a reminder that Lisa is giving away an exclusive, free spell book as a thank-you gift to new readers!

Little Book of Spells contains ten spells that are ideal for newcomers to the practice of magic, but are also suitable for any level of experience.

Read it on read on your laptop, phone, tablet, Kindle or Nook device by visiting:

www.wiccaliving.com/bonus

DID YOU ENJOY
WICCA LIVING A MAGICAL LIFE?

Thanks so much for reading this book! I know there are many great books out there about Wicca, so I really appreciate you choosing this one.

If you enjoyed the book, I have a small favor to ask—would you take a couple of minutes to leave a review for this book on Amazon?

Your feedback will help me to make improvements to this book, and to create even better ones in the future. It will also help me develop new ideas for books on other topics that might be of interest to you. Thanks in advance for your help!

CPSIA information can be obtained
at www.ICGtesting.com
Printed in the USA
LVHW090218231220
674948LV00009B/102

9 781912 715169